COMPARATIVE POLITICS

DR. BANTI KUMAR

Made with ♥ on the Notion Press Platform
www.notionpress.com

Dedicated to our sister Late Ujla Devi

Contents

Preface

With the blessing of God we have completed this book entitled *'Comparative Politics'* for the students of all Indian Universities in general and University of Jammu, University of Kashmir and Cluster University, Jammu in particular. This book has been designed according to new syllabus of B.A. Choice Based Credit Semester System of University of Jammu and Cluster University Jammu. This book also provides multiple choice questions at the end of every Chapter which will help the students to clear the entrance exams.

This book is for Semester 4th. This book consists of four chapters. This book has been designed according to the need of the students so that they can easily understand the topic and pass out their class with good marks. It also provides some political thinkers which are very important in comparative politics so that student can get a book basic idea about thinkers.

This book use very simple language so that the student community could me served better.

Acknowledgements

Firstly we would like to thanks Chound Mata, the tribal goddess of Gaddi Tribe for blessing us with a great work. We are thankful to our guide Prof. B. L. Sah, Director UGC-HRDC Kumaun University Nainital Uttrakhand for helping us in our research work. We are also thankful to our parents and other family members for their moral as well as financial support. We are also thankful to our teachers Master Kans Kumar and Sh. Sishpaul (Accounts Officer) for guiding us. We are also thankful to all our colleagues from Department of Political Science, DSB Campus Kumaun University Naintial. We are thankful to Principal Sir and our other colleague from Govt. Degree PG College Bhaderwah and member from library for making available some good books in library. We are also grateful to Prof. Neeta Bora HOD Department of Political Science, Prof. Devya Upadhaya, Prof. Madhurendra Kumar, Prof. Kalpna, Dr. Hirdesh Kumar and Dr. Bhumika Prasad from Kuman University, Nainital, Uttrakhand. We are also thankful to Prof. Bhavnaish Chand Principal Govt Degree College Dudu Basantgarh, Prof. Anil Khajuria, Principal Govt. Degree College Paddar and Mr. Kuljesh Kumar, Junior Assistant General Administration department for their valuable support. We are very thankful to hub of our friends including Mrs Anoupa Devi, Dr. Pawan Kumar, Dr. Anita Garwal and Dr. Sumit Rana. Last but not least we are also thankful to Notion Press Media Pvt. Ltd. for providing us the platform to publish this book.

CHAPTER ONE

Comparative Politics

Comparative Politics:

Introduction: As the word indicates comparative Politics is that branch of political science which deals with study of different societies by comparing them. If involves conscious comparison in studying political experiences, behaviour of political structure and process of the government in a comprehensive manner. It also includes the study of extra constitutional agencies, NGOs, Pressure groups, political parties etc. which directly or indirectly influence the functioning of the government.

As we know this world is diverse. Comparative Politics helps us to know about political diversity of this world. Aristotle was the first scholar who studied 158 constitutions of Greek city states to know about the political diversity of Greece on this basis he also gave his classification of government. He is also known as father of comparative politics.

Before the 2nd world War, Western countries i.e. the developed world was the main focus of study in comparative politics. As the third world countries (Asia and African) government independence, this focus of comparative politics changed from developed Nations to developing Nations.

Definitions:

According to M Curtis, "Comparative politics is concerned with significant regularities, similarities and differences in the working of political institutions and political behaviour."

According to E.A Freeman, "Comparative Politics is comparative analysis of the various forms of government and diverse political institutions".

According to Jean Blondel, "Comparative Politics is the study of pattern of national government in a contemporary world".

According to G. M. Smith, "It is the study of the forms of political organization their properties, correlations, variations and modes of change".

Scope of Comparative Politics: As comparative Politics is a sub field of Political science but its scope is much more and it is expanding day by day. Since the time of Aristotle its scope can be summed in following points.

a. **Study of Constitution:** It studies the constitution of different countries. By comparing it we can correct the unsuccessful provision in our constitution, which will lead to development of society. Constitution of India and China are its live examples.

b. **Study of System of Government:** By comparative politics we can study the system of government of a particular country. By comparing President Type of governments, parliament government etc we can chose the successful one.

c. **Study of Political Institution:** Comparative politics studies the different political institutions of different countries which lead to the choosing of correct successful political institution i.e. planning commission was borrowed with inspiration from Russia and NITI Ayog was established with inspiration from China.

d. **Study of political Parties:** Comparative politics studies the different political parties of different countries. In USA we have two party systems, in communist countries we have communist party only and in India we have multi-party system. By comparing them we can conclude and suggest the successful system in a particular country.

e. **Inter-disciplinary Focus:** Comparative politics accepts the desire of inter-disciplinary focus. It accepts the needs of the study of politics with the help of the knowledge of psychology, sociology, anthropology, economics and other social sciences.

f. **Empirical study of Politics:** Comparative politics studies gave more stress on empirical reach. It is no longer limited to descriptive study. It seeks to analyse, empirical and analytically the actual activities of the government.

g. **Emphasis on the study of infrastructure of politics:** Comparative politics now seeks to analyse the actual behaviour of individual, groups, structure and substructure. It is not confined to the study of former structure of the government in terms of legal power and function. It seeks to analyse their behaviour in the environment.

h. **Political Culture:** It studies the political culture of different countries. It makes a difference between their cultures such as Japanese are peace loving people where as Indians, Pakistanis as well as Bangladeshis are not as compared to Japan as they follow corrupt practices during elections.

a. **Political socialization:** It studies how people get civilized for a particular political system. Family, school as well as work place and surrounding atmosphere shapes their political behaviour. After learning in these institutions they get civilized.

j. **Political recruitment:** Different countries follow different process for political recruitment depending upon its ideology. Comparative Politics studies how people get recruited in a particular system.

k. **Human Nature:** It is very important to study as war and peace both depends upon the nature of involving parties. Comparative Politics studies this crucial matter of politics.

Evolution of Comparative Politics: Aristotle gave his classification of government by studying 158 different constitutions of City states. He supposed to be first thinker of comparative politics. So comparative politics starts from the time of Aristotle and after him Machiavelli, Tocqueville, Bryce, Organski and Weber also contributed to this field. The study of comparative politics become highly significant in 1950s when a good number of leading American political scientists thought to transfer the field of politics. They transferred it from the study of government to the study of political process. David Easton, Jean Blondel, Gabriel Almond and Robert Dhal also contributed in this field.

Differentiate between Comparative Government and Comparative Politics

Comparative Government

a. It is older than comparative politics.
b. It depends upon classical approaches i.e. philosophical, Historical, and legal approaches.
c. It has been oriented toward European politics.
d. It focuses theory building on the basis of idealism.
e. It ignores inter-disciplinary approach.
f. Its scope is narrow.
g. It focuses directly into Government.
h. Its goal is description.
a. It is a basic concept.

Comparative Politics

a. It is younger than comparative government.
b. It depends upon modern approaches, i.e. scientific empirical and behavioural methods, structural functional approach.
c. It is oriented towards all including developed and developing countries.
d. Scientific theory building was its main motive.
e. It focuses on inter-disciplinary approach.
f. Its scope is wider.
g. It also focuses on environment effecting Government.
h. Its goal is explanation.
a. It is an improvement in the concept of comparative government.

Conclusion: It can be concluded from the above discussion that comparative government and comparative politics both deals with comparative study of the Nations. Various thinkers have treated them same. Comparative politics is an updated version of comparative government. This update is same as we see in political science i.e. from idealism to realism. Comparative government was biased toward European politics but comparative politics treats all the regions developed, developing and under-developed equally.

Political System model by David Easton/System Approach (David Easton)

The system theory had its origin in the Natural sciences. It was first of all given by German biologist Ludwing Von Bertalanffy. After its development through Anthropology and sociology it was applied to political science by David Easton. The system approach favours an interdisciplinary approach. According to it in order to understand a system we must have to understand the functioning of its each unit which contribute in the functioning of system. After the introduction of this approach in Political science by David Easton, it was further developed by various thinkers such as Gabriel Almond, Karl Deutsch etc.

Definitions:

According to David Easton, "Political system is that behaviour or set up interaction through which authoritative allocation of values are made and implemented for society."

According to Ludwing Von Bertalanffy, "A system is a set of elements standing in interaction".

According to Hall and Fagen, "A political system is a set of objects together with relation between the objects and between their attitudes".

According to Colin Chery, "A system is a whole which is composed of many parts an ensemble of attitudes".

David Easton had introduced the concept of Political system in his work 'The Analysis of Political System' published in 'world politics' in 1957.

The political system approach as given by David Easton is shown below.

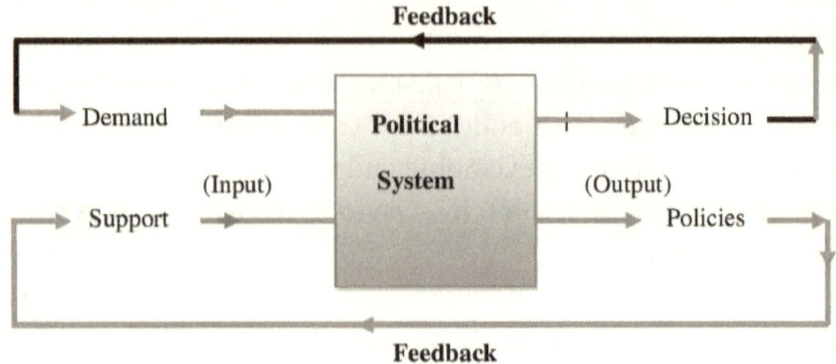

System model of David Easton

Components of diagram are shown below:-

a. **Input:** A political system takes input in the form of support and demands. It is very important because on its basis a political system gives its demand. Demands can be of four types **i.e.** Demands for allocation of goods, Demands for regulation of behaviour, Demands for participation of political system, Demand for communication and information. Demands have their origin either in environment of the system or within system. David Easton calls them external and internal demands respectively. Demands from social environment, cultural environment, ecological environment etc are external demands. Internal demands emerge from the internal of a system may be to change a system. Supports are those structures or processes which give the political system the capacity to cope with demands made upon it. Support means giving obedience and showing loyalty to a political system. Supports are classified into two types. Overt Support and Covert Support.Overt refers to the actions that are clearly and manifestly supportive. Covert

Support refers to supportive attitude or sentiments.

b. **Regulatory Mechanism:** Every political system possesses regulatory mechanisms of its own to prevent the demands from entering into the system. Regulatory mechanisms are Structural Mechanisms, Cultural Mechanism, Communication Channels and Reduction Processes. Structural Mechanisms are also known as gatekeepers e.g. Pressure groups, political parties etc. Cultural Mechanism is the demands against culture remain unaccepted and are not articulated. Communication Channels areDemands gets scattered widely with a number of communication channels and hence get diluted. Reduction Processes includesLegislators, executive and administrative bodies to filter the demands according to their importance.

c. **Output:** An output of a Political system is a political decision or policy. Decision is on a particular issue and policy is a long time effect. Output is also important for the survival of the system because it has its direct effect on the public i.e. its supporters. It is depended upon the input received by system.

d. **Feedback:** Easton describes it as feedback loop. An output has its effect on the public and the public supports the political system based on its output. This attitude of public toward the political system after analyzing its output is called feedback. It is very important because it changes the system according to the need of the people.

Political Economy and Dependency Approach (A G Frank)

Political Economy: Matters related to the production and distribution of the goods has an economic character. In order to do a fair production and distribution in the society the state makes some restriction on the process of production and distribution. For the proper development of a country it is necessary to makes its economy strong. This inter-dependence of the polity and economy is called political economy. During ancient times economy was also treated as an important activity of the states by king. It is necessary to have more wealth to bear the loss of war and maintain a large standing army for defiance of the state. They use to collect revenue as tax from agriculture income of the citizens.

The invention of the agriculture forced the human being to settle at a fixed place. The production of surplus agriculture products lead to the invention of barter system. Still further development in this field lead to money in form of coins. During this stage in order to make exchange fair and equal these economic activities was put under the control of the state. In the field of political economy the discussion on the control of state on economic matter lead to the emergency of school of liberalism, Socialism and communism. A large number of thinkers such as J.S Mill, Karl Marks, Mitchell, Schumpeter and Freedman etc contributed in the field.

The classical liberal thinkers supported that there should not be the control of state in economic field. The supported a lazes fair policies, they treated state as necessary evil, they believe that should provide only security. The modern liberal thinkers believe in welfare state, they favoured interventions of state in the economic activities to do welfare of the people.

Karl Marx favoured that production and distribution should be under the control of worker class. In the contemporary world political economy is an integral part of every political system. In democratic countries every economic activities is under the control of government. Government levies taxes on import, export, selling and buying etc and these activities are a source of income for the state. Democratic countries also favour privatization in order to develop the large sectors.

In communist countries the government also control the economic sectors but private players are not welcomed as seen in democratic countries. More over communist countries are also getting attracted toward mixed economy and are performing better. People Republic of China is its live example.

<u>Dependency Approach:</u> It is an attempt to explain the root causes of underdevelopment of third world countries and makes the developed countries directly responsible for their under development. This model is advocated by *Andre Gunder Frank,*

Nallestein, Celso Furtado etc.

The concept of dependency is widely used in comparative analysis of third world political system in Latin America, Asia and Africa. It evolved in Latin America in the 1960's and was later discussed in some writing about Asia and Africa as well. Both liberal and Marxist writer have propounded their own versions of the phenomena of development and underdevelopment resulting in considerable theoretical confusion about the nature of dependency and its conceptual implications.

Lenin was the first to refer to the concept of dependency as a part of his general theory of imperialism. He understood capitalist imperialism as a manifestation of the struggle among the colonial powers for the economic and political division of the world. Several Marxist thinkers explain under development of dependent countries by referring to dominants of the third world countries by monopoly capitalism. These writers argued that today corporate capitalism has replaced financial capital as the instrument of dominance in the dependent countries.

Marini has propounded the theory of sub-imperialism regarding capitalist development in Brazil. He characterised Brazilian capitalism as super-exploitive, with a rapid accumulation benefiting to the owner of means of production and absolute poverty securing to masses. His approach combined a dependency perspective with a Marxist anti imperialist framework.

A G Frank provides another frame work for dependency theory, he emphasised commercial monopoly rather than feudalism and pre-capitalist forms is the economy means where by national and regional metropolises exploit and appropriate surplus from the satellites. Thus capitalism own world scale promotes developing metropolises at the expenses of under development and dependents satellites. Other theorists of dependency believe that an independent capitalist development was not feasible and that instead socialism must be introduce along with a planned political economy and an intensive utilisation of natural resources. However there is no popular moment for socialism.

Objective Type Questions

1. The system approach in political science was given by

a. David Easton
b. Gabriel Almond
c. Hall and Fagon
d. None of the above

1. The system approach was first of all given by

a. Gabriel Almond
b. Lucian Pye
c. Ludwing Van Bertalanfy
d. None of the above

3. 'A system analysis of political life' was written by

a. J. S. Mill
b. Edward Shills
c. Herbert Spenser
d. David Easton

4. 'The Politics of Developing Areas' was written by

a. Gabriel Almond
b. David Easton
c. Almond and Verba
d. Lucien W. Pye

5. The stages of Political Development was written by

a. Bentham
b. Kenth Organsci
c. Lucian Pye

d. None of the Above

6. 'Comparative Politics: A Developmental approach' was written by

a. C. W. Mill
b. J. S. Mill
c. Almond and Powell
d. None of the above

7. The Concept of '*Gate Keepers*' was given by

a. Mahatma Gandhi
b. Arbindo Ghosh
c. J. P. Narayan
d. David Easton

8. The concept of '*Encoding and Decoding*' was given by

a. J. P. Narayan
b. Karl Deutsch
c. J. S. Mill
d. None of the above

9. Match the followings

a. Gabriel Almond 1. USA
b. David Easton 2. England
c. Lucian Pye 3. USA
d. Karl Marx 4. Germany

    a b c d
    A 1 3 2 4
    B 1 2 3 4
    C 4 3 2 1

D 3 4 1 2

10. 'The Civic Culture: Political Attitude and Democracy in Nations' was written by

a. Gabriel Almond and Verbha
b. David Easton.
c. J. L. Palombra
d. None of the above

Answer key

1. **(a)** 2. **(c)** 3. **(d)** 4. **(a)** 5. **(b)** 6. **(c)** 7 **(d)** 8. **(b)** 9. **(a)** 10. **(a)**

CHAPTER TWO

Political Process and Political Development

Political Culture: Meaning, Types and Determinants

After the birth of a human being, he continuously learns the Principles, rules and regulations of society in order to become a civilized human being. These rules and regulations are called culture. The concept of culture was first of all introduced by a British Anthropologist E. B. Taylor to Anthropology in 1871. He defined it as 'That complex whole which includes knowledge, belief, art, morals, law customs and any other capabilities and habits acquired by man as member of society'.

Political culture is one of the dimensions of the culture. This concept is new in the discipline of Political science. This concept also emerged in the field of political science between the two world wars. It was first introduced by Gabriel A Almond in his research paper titled '*Comparative Political System*' published in 1956.

Definitions:

"The pattern of individual attitudes and orientations towards politics among the members of a political system" **Almond and Powell**

"A political culture is composed of the attitude beliefs, emotions and value of society"

Dennis Kavanagh

"Political culture is a pattern of ideas and Traditions about authority" **Samul Beer**

"Political culture is made up of shared goals and community accepted rules of individual and group interactions" **Roy Macridis**

Types of Political Culture: Based upon the orientation of of individual toward their political system, Almond and Verba gave following three types

a. **Parochial Political Culture:** In this type people have no or less awareness about their political system. They have no awareness about output process of their government. They are not interested to play any role. This type of political culture is found in every society. It is more in traditional societies and less in developed western societies. There is no specialisation i.e. legislative, executive, judiciary or economic process e.g. Headman, African Chiefdoms etc.

b. **Subject Political Culture:** In this type people have knowledge about their political system. They know about various government roles e.g. collection of taxes, law making etc. But they are not interested to take active part in it. They don't have clear knowledge of the way in which they can influence the political system e.g. monarchical government etc.

c. **Participant Political Culture:-** In this type people aware about their political system. They take active part in input as well as in output of political system. They treat themselves as an integral part of political system. This culture is seen in highly developed societies particularly in western democratic countries. There is specialization of functions such as legislative, executive, judiciary, economy etc work by experts of their fields.

In addition to these three they also gave following sub classes of culture.

a. **Political sub-culture:** It may be possible that entire population of political system may not have the same political culture. Some section of population may have parochial, other have participant still other have subject political culture.

b. **Mass Culture:** The culture followed by the ruled section of population is called mass culture.

c. **Elite Culture:** The culture followed by the ruling class is called elite culture.

d. **The Civic Culture:** In order to know about the difference between culture of Nations, Almond and Verba studied 5000 peoples in five different countries i.e. USA, Britain, West Germany, Italy and Mexico between 1959 and 1960. After the study and analysis of data they came to know that the people in the USA participate more in the functioning of government as compared to other countries. They are emotionally involved in their political system and have a high degree of respect for civic participation. The British people are too attached with their political system but less than Americans. In Italy people are alienated from political system same in the case with Mexican political system. German has trust on their political system and hence avoids more participation. On the basis of above study Almond and Verba put this concept of civic culture. In this type of political culture People though governed through their elected representatives, keep on taking active part in various processes of politics. This type of culture is shown by American political system.

Determinants of Political Culture: Various factors which are responsible for the growth of a particular culture are known as determinants of a political culture. Following are some of the determinants of political culture.

a. **Historical Factor:** The history of a country is responsible for the growth of a particular culture. Various historical events such as French revolution, American Revolution, Magna Carta, Glorious Revolution, Total Revolution and Chinese revolution have shaped the culture of respective countries.

b. **Political continuity and Discontinuity:** The continuity of political process helps in achieving participant political culture and discontinuity helps in its degradation.

c. **Geography:** It is most important factor for promotion of political culture. Favourable location of Britain helped her to save her culture but the unsuitable location of India is responsible for her diversities.

d. **Socio- Economic Factor:** It plays an important role in laying down the foundation of a political culture. Level of poverty, employment, literacy, urbanization plays an important role in motivating the population to participate in political system.

e. **Ethnic Factor:** This factor is responsible for laying down the foundation of strong sub political culture within the national political culture. It is due to the illiteracy and diversity in the population in the country. It is seen in Indian political system because of the linguistic and religious diversity.

f. **Ideological Factor:** Ideology motivates the citizens to take part in political system. Communist countries alienate their population from the participation in political system and hence lay down foundation of parochial political culture. Democratic countries motivate their citizens to participate in political system and hence make a progress in the attainment of civil culture.

Political Participation: Meaning, Types and determinations

Political Participation: The act of taking part in an event or activity is called participation. The act of taking part in a political event or political activity is called political participation. It refers to the involvement of the people in decision making, policy formulation, electoral process and the struggle for power in the society. It includes all activities through which the people get involved in the political process. It does not mean merely the exercise of right to vote by the people. It refers to their active involvement in the decision making process of the political system.

Political participation is an integral part of every political system. Democracy completely survives on it. No political system can work without securing the performance of political role by the people. Political participation refers to any of the many ways in which people seek to influence the composition or policies of their government. It can be supporting policies and decision of government. It can be supporting policies and decision of government opposing it or even engaging terrorist act against the state.

Definitions

"Political Participation is the involvement of the member of society in the decision making process" -------- **Almond and Powell**

"Political Participation is the involvement of masses in the decision making process or policy formulation" ------ **Heinz Eulau**

"Political Participation is the movement of the individual at various levels in the political system" -------**Michael Rush and Philip Althoff**

Types of Political Participation: Different scholars have offered different types of political participation. Some important among them are given below.

a. **Direct Political Participation:** In this type people play a direct role in the election of their rulers and in the decision making or policy formulation process.

b. **Indirect Political System:** In this type people elect their representatives directly and through these take part in decision making indirectly.

c. **Active Political Participation:** In this type people actively participate in the political process, leadership - recruitment, elections, political communication, political parties and pressure group activities.

d. **Low or Passive Political Participation:** When the people have little interest in the political process it is called passive political participation.

e. **Instrumental Political Participation:** In this type people participate in politics with definite ends with a view they want to achieve in politics.

f. **Expressive Political Participation:** In this type people participate in politics without any commitment to a definite objective but for the satisfaction of their feelings.

g. **Political Participation through Legitimate Means:** In this type people participate in the political process through legitimate and constitutional means.

h. **Political Participation through illegitimate means:** In this type people participate in politics through non-constitutional means such as violence, riots and protest etc.

Levels of Participation: Following thinkers have given some level of participation

a. Wood and Roper gave four levels i.e. very active, active, inactive and very active.

b. Robert Dahl divided the citizens into two types as apolitical stratum and political stratum on the basis of their participation in politics. Apolitical are those which are not interested and political are those which are interested. He again divided the political stratum into power seeker and powerful.

Determinations of Political Participation: The Role that people of a political system play in the political process particularly in decision making, policy formulation is influenced by several factors such as Psychological, Social, Economy, Political and Environmental etc. These are referred as the determinants of political participation. Some of them are explained below-

a. **Psychological Factors:** Desire for power and value has always motivated people to get involved in political process. Many people find the political field useful for getting them opportunity for winning in election and hence access to all powerful resources.

b. **Social Factors:** Education, sex, age caste Religion, language affects the political participation of the citizens.

c. **Political Factors:** The system of governance affects the participation of the citizens. A democratic government tries to acquire mass political participation whereas a communist system is against it.

d. **Economic Factors:** The expectation of rewards in terms of economic gains attracts the individual to participate in political process. They went to become part of decision making and policy formulation which favour them.

e. **Environment Factor:** It motivates to participate or not in a political system. It there is political participation in surrounding, an individual will also show political participation.

f. **Nature of Citizens:** If the citizens are revolutionary, they will participate in political process during good as well as bad days e.g. Citizens of Ukraine are helping their state against Russia.

Political Socialization: Meaning and Agents

Political Socialization:-The process by which we learn the political culture is known as Political Socialization. It includes all formal, informal, deliberate and unplanned learning at every state of life. The term '*Political Socialization*' was first of all coined by an American sociologist H. H. Hyman. After Hyman various political scientists such as Lasswell, Easton, Hass, Almond and Verba use this concept for study of various phenomena of politics. Political socialization is very crucial for the stability of government.

Political socialization is a part of socialization in general. It represents the political dimension of the socialization process. It is a process by which people of a society learn values, believes, norms and goals of their cultures. Political culture is a psychological concept whereas political socialization is a sociological concept. Political socialization is a universal concept. It is responsible for transmitting political culture from one generation to another.

Definitions:-

According to Almond and Powell, "Political Socialization is the process by which Political culture are maintained and changed".

According to David Easton, "Political Socialization is that developmental process by which Political cultures are maintained and changed".

According to Allan R Ball, "Political Socialization is the establishment and development of attitudes and beliefs about the Political System".

According to Dennis Kavanagh, "Political socialization is used to describe the process whereby individual learns and develops orientation to politics".

According to Robert Lenin, "Political socialization is the means by which individuals acquire motives, habits and Values relevant to participation in a political system".

Types of Political Socialization: According to Almond and Powell, Political Socialization is of following two types-

a. **Manifest Political Socialization:** It is manifest when certain values, or felling towards political system are put into the minds of others directly, clearly and manifestly e.g. Respect for authority, knowledge about rights and biased toward a particular ideology etc. usually formal method such as education institutions, use of mass media, lectures are used in it. It is also known as direct Political socialization.

b. **Latent Political Socialization:-** It is the transmission of non-political attitudes which affect attitudes toward political roles, objects and political system. It includes those socialization processes which indirectly affect the political socialization. Eg. Submission to the authority of father makes the children to accept the political authority in future. Following the rules and regulations of a family prepares the individual to follow the rules of political system. It is also known as indirect political socialization.

In addition to above there are following types

a. Particularistic Political socialization: In it individual is taught only one role.

b. Universalistic Political socialization: In it individual is taught several roles.

c. Affective Political socialization: In it stress is given on emotional values and loyalties etc.

Agents of Political Socialization

Those institutions, groups or relations with the help of which we learn political culture is called agents of political socialization. Following are some of important agents of political socialization.

a. **Family:** It is the first state through every individual passes. In this unit every individual keeps learning from birth to death. Here individual comes in contact with authority and decision making process, security etc.

b. **School:** This is the second most powerful agent after family. It also acts as a bridge between family and society. Different opportunities in the school prepare the individual for his struggle in life.

c. **Employment experiences:** After the school it plays an important part in the field of political socialization. Here individual comes in contact with authority and responsibility. In this state all his theoretical experienced gets a practical shape.

d. **Religion:** Particularly in under-developed and developing countries, it plays an important part. Reading religious text books, attending religious gathering in Temple Mosque etc also helps in political socialization.

e. **Mass Media:** An individual is the reflection of his environment. Radio, TV, Newspaper social media provides the suitable environment to the individuals. It also helps in shaping the level of political socialization.

f. **Participation in Political System:** Contract of individual with Political parties, pressure group, knowledge of form of government etc. also important of agent of political socialization.

Political Development: Concept and Ingredients

Development is the process in which something or some grows or changes and becomes more advanced. It is a multi dimensional process of change. The political dimension of development is called political development. Before 1950 Anthropologist, Sociologist, Historian used to study the colonial nations of Asia and Africa. As these nations emerged as independent states after 1950, American political scientists started the study of political dynamics of these newly emerged states. These countries were not developed and after independence they started developing themselves. After the American social scientists curiosity became popular and various thinkers offered its definition.

Definitions:

According to S. P. Huntington, "Political development is institutionalization of political organization and procedure".

According to Edward Shills, "Political development is nation state building".

According to W.W Ruston, "Political development is a typical phenomenon of industrial societies".

According to Daniel Learner, "Political development is passage of ancient societies and the modernization of middle east".

Various thinkers such as Edward shills, Coleman, F. W. Riggs, Almond, Talcott Parsons and Deutsch have given concept of political development. Lucian Pye an American Political scientist after analysis of various thinkers gave three characteristics of political development as Equality Capacity, Differentiation and Specialisation and these are explained below;

a. **Equality:** A basic characteristic of political development is attitude toward equality. It not includes only mass participation and popular involvement in Political activities but the law should be universalistic nature i.e. applicable to all. It also includes equality among national citizens, legal order and role allocation.

b. **Capacity:** It refers to the capacity of a political system by which it can give output and influence more population. It is the capacity with which a government can change social and economic condition of its citizens. It also includes the effectiveness and efficiency in the execution of public policy, rationality in administration and a secular orientation toward policy.

c. **Differentiation and Specialization:** This aspect promotes the differentiation and specialization of the government. Offices and agencies must have their distinct and limited function. There must be division of responsibility and specialization of function. The division of power should be integrated so that the whole system works by integration and specialization.

F.W Riggs agrees with the three characteristics of political development. He declared that there should be balance between equality, capacity and differentiation otherwise the political system will get caught in a ***development trap.*** With this the political system will experience political decay or break down.

S.P Huntington defines political development as institutionalisation of political organization and procedure. Political development can occur only if Political procedure and organizations are given shape of institutions. He further argues that what is going in third world today is not political development but political decay.

Eisenstadt gives concept of political breakdown. He says that third world countries have copied the institutions from developed west and these are not fit to the condition of these third world countries. It is leading to military rule, revolution etc.

David Apter gives two stages of development i.e. Pre-industrial state and Post industrial state.

J.P Nettle and Leonard Binder have also contributed to concept of Political development.

Ingredients of Political Development: These are the indicators which indicate us about the development of a state. Some of the important ingredients are mentioned below.

a. **Territorial Integration:** It is the most important ingredient of Political development as it is directly linked with the survival of Political system. An integral state is not easily invaded by the foreign ruler and hence there will be continuous growth.

b. **Military Expenditure:** To maintain a standing are more funds should be allotted to military. By having a strong army a state uses the strategy of power politics to achieve growth.

c. **Education System:** System of education and literacy rate of a state also shows the level of her development. The more literacy rate, the higher is development.

d. **Universal Adult Franchise:** The Right to vote is also important for progress of a state. States having right to votes are supposed to be more developed than others.

e. **Ideology:** On an average basis in the world, Democracy is supposed to be more developed. States having democratic system are supposed to be more developed.

f. **Freedom of Press:** It is also a feature of developed state. For the proper development of a political system, freedom of press is necessary.

g. **Secularism:** It is also important for the development of political system. Secular states develop more as compared to theocratic states.

h. **Decentralisation:** To transfer the decision making authority to low level is called decentralization. It is very important to making more citizens a part of decision making. It is also an important ingredient of political development.

Objective Type Questions

1. Who among the following coined the term 'Political Socialism'?

a. Gabriel Almond
b. H H Hymen

c. J. S. Mill

d. None of the above

1. Gabriel Almond borrowed majority of his philosophy from

a. J. S. Mill

b. Bentham

c. Talcott Person

d. None of the above

3. The work *'The Civic Culture'* belongs to which of the following authors

a. G. Almond & Sydney Verba

b. J. S. Mill & Bentham

c. Plato & Aristotle

d. Thakur Frank Das & Rajni Kothari

4. *The Civic Culture* is based on the study of which of the following countries

a. China, India, Pakistan, Bangladesh, Sri Lanka

b. USA, U.K, Mexico, Germany, Italy

c. N. Korea, Russia, China, Taiwan, S. Korea

d. None of the above

5. Which among the following thinkers first used the word *'Civic Culture Word'*?

a. Gabriel Almond

b. Peter Lasslet

c. George Sabine

d. Rosa Luxemberg

6. Who defined Political Parties as *'Vanguard of Democracy'*?

a. Smith
b. Munro
c. Zoya Hassan
d. None of the above

7. Who among the following wrote *'Development Theory'*?

a. Maurice Duverger
b. Giovomin Sartori
c. J. L. Palombra
d. None of the above

8. *'Circulation of elite'* is the famous work of which of the following authors

a. Pareto
b. Mill
c. Mosca
d. None of the above

9. Who among the following gave the concept of *'Political Decay'*

a. Pareto
b. S. P. Huntington
c. Mao
d. Lenin

10. The *Polyarchial Democracy* is a great work of

a. Robert A. Dhal
b. Mill
c. Pareto
d. None of the above

11. Who is the author of work *'A System Analysis of Political Life'*?

a. Talcott Person
b. Gabriel Almond
c. David Easton
d. Robert Dahl

12. Comparative Politics Today was written by which of the following author

a. S. P. Huntington
b. David Apter
c. C. W. Mill
d. G. K. Roberts

13. *'The Process of Government'* was written by

a. C. W. Mill
b. Pareto
c. Arthur Bentley
d. None of the above

14. *'Elite Theory of Democracy'* was given by

a. Gabriel Almond
b. Robert Michels
c. Maurice Duverger
d. J. S. Banks

15. Who wrote the *'Comparative Politics: A Development Approach'*

a. Gabriel Almond
b. Talcott Person
c. A. R. Radcliffe Brown
d. None of the above

Answer key

1. (b) 2. (c) 3. (a) 4. (b) 5. (a) 6. (a) 7 (c) 8. (a)
9. (b) 10. (a) 11.(c) 12.(d) 13.(c) 14.(a) 15.(a)

CHAPTER THREE

Political Dynamics: Democracy, Electoral Process and Party System

Theories of Democracy: Elitist and Pluralist

Democracy: This term is derived from two Greek words i.e. '*demos*' which means people and '*Kratien*' which means rule. So democracy means the rule by the people. The word 'democracy' was first used by Greek historian Herodotus in 5th century for rule by the people. Abraham Lincoln defined democracy as "government of the people, by the people, for the people".

Elitist Theory of Democracy

Elite theories were originally developed in the field of sociology to explain the behaviour of men in his society. They believe that in every society there are two categories of people a minority which holds a special status as well as special power and privilege and a majority which accepts the decisions of the minority. The majority does not hold special social status as well as power. The concept of elite can be traced to ancient western political thought in the writing of Plato who advocates a philosopher ruler for his ideal state. Aristotle also contributed in it by saying that some men are born for rule and others to be ruled.

In modern times the concept of elite was given by two scholars Gaetano Mosca in his work '*The ruling class*' and Robert Michels in

'Political Parties: A sociological study of the oligarchies Tendencies of Modern Democracy'. Vilfredo Pareto was the first thinker to use the word *'Elite'* in his work ***The Mind and Society***. The concept of elite theory is against the concept of Democracy which says that government is of the people by the people and for the people. The elite theorist believes that democracy is a government not by people but by some elite.

Robert Michel propounded his famous concept *Iron Law of oligarchy* which implied that every organization is eventually reduced to an oligarchy that is the rule of chosen few based on their manipulative skills. Majority of human beings are apathetic, indolent, and slavish and they are permanently incapable of self government.

In order to defend the theory of democracy against the criticism by elite theorist, contemporary Theorist of democracy updated it and named it as Elite theory of democracy. Following are the some of the scholars who made a good contribution in the field of elite theory of democracy.

Karl Mannheim: He argued that society did not cease to be democratic by entrusting the actual shaping of the policy to the elites. The people cannot directly participate in the government, but they can make their aspirations felt at certain intervals, which is sufficient for the democracy. In a democracy the government can always act to remove their leaders or forces them to take decisions in the interest of the many. He stresses more on selection of elites by merit and shortening of distance between elites and the masses for successful democratic government.

Schumpeter: He was of the view that the forms of government should be distinguished by their institutions and especially by their method of appointing and dismissing the supreme makers of law and policy. Democratic method is that institutional arrangement for arriving at political decisions in which individuals acquire the power to decide by a competitive struggle through winning more votes. Democracy is not a government of the people, nor it is a means to give effect to the will of the people, nor it is a means to give effect to the will of the people, rulers comprise a select group of individual who may be distinguished from the common people. Role of common people is reduced to choosing their rules from the competing elites. The important feature of democracy is that unlike other forms of government it doesn't allow the political leadership to wield absolute power.

Raymond Aron: According to him liberal democracy is characterized by a general system of checks and balances and plurality of elites. He points out that soviet society is distinguished by a unified elite belonging to communist party whereas the western society is characterized by divided elite which makes it pluralistic society. According to this theory if power remains in the hands of elite class but it is balanced by a sound opposition and the masses are also left to play an important role by selecting the elite class and even pressurize them in their functioning.

Giovanni Sartori gave his views in his work "Democratic theory". He regards democracy as a procedure in which leaders complete at elections for authority to govern. The role of elite does not suggest any imperfection of democracy on the other hand it is core of the democratic system. Any notion of self governing people is a delusion. The real danger to democracy emanates not from the existence of leadership i.e. elite but from the absence of the elite.

<u>**Pluralist Theory of Democracy**</u>

Pluralism: It is a belief in the diversity or multiplicity in society. It is used to denote the existence of party competition, multiplicity of ethnic values or a variety of culture norms. It is a theory of the distribution of political power. It holds that Power is widely and evenly dispersed in society rather than concentrated in the hands of an elite or a ruling class. It is seen as a theory of group politics in which individual are represented largely through their membership of organized groups and all such groups have access to the policy process.

Pluralist theory of Democracy: The advocates of this theory criticize the elite theory of democracy. They believe that political, economic as well as decision making power is not held by a handful minority called elite class but it is held by many groups and associations operating in a society. Public Policy as well as decision making is a result of bargaining between various associations and groups.

This Pluralist idea can be traced back to early liberal political philosophy particularly the ideas of Locke and Montesquieu. The systematic development of this idea was found in the writing of James Madison.

This concept was further developed in the writing of Robert Dahl. He pointed out that change in size of city states to modern national states inevitably lead to a shift from a monist to a pluralist democracy. This change in scale is crucial to understanding present day democracies. In the modern context, the very essence of democracy is realised by *Polyarchy* which stipulates the presence of a large number of organizations and associations. They enjoy relative autonomy both in relationship to one another with regards to government power and jurisdiction.

The advocates of this theory believe in decentralization of power. They reject the monistic idea of Hobbes and Austin. Pluralist believe that state must recognize the personality and autonomy of social groups and allow them to take part in the political process of the country. The main function of the state is to deal with social conflicts in such a way that the competitive struggle for power is regulated.

A.F Bentley and David Truman in USA interpreted democracy as a political game played by a great variety of groups. According to them, government is the focal point for public Pressure and its task is to make policies which reflect the highest common group demand. Thus democratic society is seen as a pluralist where the management of public affairs is shared by a number of groups having different values, sources and method of influence.

Pluralist theory of democracy can be criticized on the following grounds.

a. It is against the sovereign position of the state. It lays too much stress on the autonomy of different social groups which creates a danger for sovereignty of state.

b. It is against the Marxism. Marxists criticize this theory by saying that it wants to promote the present capitalist system. It preaches the autonomy for different classes but in a socialist society there is only a single class so it becomes irrelevant for a socialist society.

c. It is not suitable for third world countries as these countries are not developed politically very well. So giving such autonomy to different social groups as claimed by pluralists could lead to crash of political system.

d. Based on the real scenario of the world, modern empirical social and political scientists accept the interpretation of elite theorist.

e. In modern times because of the large population, the doctrine of pluralism has lost its significance since the Second World War. Now elite classes are playing an important role for growth of National States.

f. The concept of Pluralism is suited for a developed democracy and is harmful for a socialist system.

Polyarchy: It refers to a model of political process chiefly outlined by Robert Dahl in his work 'A preface to Democratic Theory'. It says that the policy making process in a liberal Democracy, however centralised it may appear in form, is in reality a highly decentralized process of bargaining among relatively autonomous groups. Accordingly, Public policy is an outcome of the interaction among all groups who make claims upon or express interest in a particular issue. The role of government in such a situation is little more than that of an honest broker in the middle.

<u>Theories of Representation: Territorial, Proportional and Functional</u>

Representation: The act of giving or showing something to somebody is called presentation. The act of authorizing a person, organization that speaks, act of is present officially for someone else is called representation.

During the ancient time the democracy was suitable for small states and was known as direct democracy. Citizens used to participate directly in every decision making event of government. As the population increased and the concept of democracy travelled to large states, they modified it to suit the large population. This modified version is called indirect democracy. In this version of democracy citizens used to elect their few representatives by the power of vote for a fixed period. These representatives take part directly in the decision making process of the government on behalf of the electing population.

So representation is an integral process in the functioning of democracy.

Theories of Representation:

Andrew Heywood gave following four theories of representation as described below.

1. **Trustee Model:** A trustee is a person who is vested with formal responsibility for another's property or affairs.
2. **Delegate Model:** A delegate is a person who is chosen to act for another on the basis of clear guidance or instructions.
3. **Mandate Model:** It is based on the idea that in winning on election, a party gains a popular mandate that authorises it to carry out what ever policies or programmes it had outlined during the election campaign.
4. **Resemblance Model:** It suggests that only persons coming from a particular group and who have shared the experiences of that group can fully identify with its interests.

In addition to above four following are also important theories of representation.

a. **The Reactionary theory of Representation:** It was given by Thomas Hobbles and Alexander Hamilton. They regard ruler as the best custodian of public interest. It is not a democratic theory. It accepts a limited public interest in policy making.

b. **Conservative Theory of representation:** The main exponents of this theory are Edmund Burke and James Madison. This theory allows the citizens to elect their representatives. It is an elite theory. It gives public control without encouraging popular participation

c. **Liberal Theory of Representation:** Its main exponents are John Locke and Thomas Jefferson. This theory believes in equality of all people having capacity to rule. This theory banks on the wisdom of masses and treats elite as their agents or messengers.

d. **Radical Theory of Representation:** J.J. Rousseau is its main exponents. It arose against the soviet hegemony over the international communist movement and grows stronger in 1960's.

Territorial Representation: It is also known as geographical representation. In this process the whole country is divided into geographical area of nearly equal population. These geographical areas are called constituencies. Voters of each constituency elect their representatives. The geographical area of the constituencies can be big or small but while making this division, distribution of equal population in every constituency is taken in mind.

The constituencies can be single member constituency or multi-member constituency. In single member constituency, the voters elect single representative from their constituency. In multi-member constituency, the voters elect move than one representative from their constituency.

In single member constituency mostly the first past the post and second ballot system are followed. In first past the post, the candidate scoring highest votes is declared as winner. This method is very simple and is followed in various countries including India. This method is good but sometimes the successful candidate gets less than absolute majority of votes.

Moreover it mainly focuses on proportion of population. It favours the ruling political party as it alters the boundaries of constituencies by the practice of gerrymandering. This system mostly favours large political parties. In order to avoid these problems we use second ballot system. This second ballot system is very famous in France. In France election is cancelled if no candidates gets absolute majority of votes and it is held again in which only two candidates having highest votes are allowed to contest.

For multi-member constituencies, we use proportional representation.

Proportional Representation: This system of representation was invented in the 19th century. It was adopted by European democratic countries. It is based on the principal that the percentage of seats for each party should be in direct proportion to its percentage vote share secured in election. This system is particularly adopted in multimember constituencies to secure a fair representation for both majority and minority. It has mainly two types i.e. single transferable vote system and list system.

a. **Single Transferable vote system:** This system is used for multimember constituencies. In it voters vote for candidates and not for parties. Each political party sends Candidates equal to number of seats to be filled or less. The voters vote with order of preferences of 1, 2, 3.... The winning candidates are required to achieve a quota of votes as shown below.

$$= \frac{\textit{Total number of valid votes}}{\textit{Total seats} + 1} + 1$$

It a candidate wins then his surplus votes are transferred to the other candidates by counting their 2nd preference. Even if we fail to get the required number of winner candidates by such transfer of surplus votes. The candidate with least votes is excluded from the list and the 2nd preference of his voters is counted. This process continues till we get number of required winning candidates. This method is also use for elections to Rajya Sabha as multiple member constituencies. Moreover it is used for our state legislative council. The method of single transferable vote system was first given by Danish Minister Carl Andrae in1793. It was modified and improved by Thomas Hare of England in 1951.

b. **List System:** This system is used for either multimember constituency or single national constituency. In this method, voters vote for a party and not for individual candidate. Some countries follow closed list system which means voters vote only for party with no preference on hierarchy of candidates. Some countries also follow open list system which means they also provide the voters the choice to change hierarchy of the competing candidates. In the list system seats are distributed among the political parties based on their share of secured votes. For example if there are 100 seats and a political party secures 30% of total votes casted. So this party will get 30 seats out of 100. These 30 seats will be given to top 30 candidates as declared by some political party in closed list system. These 30 seats will be given to top 30 preferred candidates in open list system.

Functional Representation: In contemporary times, every society includes workers, peasants, traders, teachers, doctors, lawyers and other specialized persons in their field. These persons have a diversity of interest. Keeping in view this diversity the social scientists gave another method known as Functional Representation.

This method advocates that people belonging to different occupations or functions should be allowed to elect their representatives on functional basis. These representatives should make decisions related to their specific functions. For instance those belonging to industry should vote on industrial policy. Those belonging to sports should vote on sports policy etc.

The champions of functional representation argue that the representatives of a particular Territory cannot take care of the interest of all sections of the people living in that territory. So the people should send their representatives to decision making bodies on the basis of their specific economic and professional interest and not on a territorial basis. The guild socialists of Britain are strong supporter of this system of representation.

Party System: One Party, Bi-party and Multi-party system

Political parties are the most important agencies that participate in political process in a modern state. It can be defined as organized group of people, having a clear ideology and based upon a certain well defined polices. It is a binding of people in the form of association with a motive to capture the power of government. Different scholars have offered different definitions of political parties. Some of them are given below.

A Political party is 'a body of men united for promoting the national interest on some particular principles in which they all are agreed'. **Burke**

A Political Party is 'a group of men banded together to pursue certain principles' **Disraeli**

A Political Party is 'a group of men professing the same political doctrine' **Benjamin Constant**

A Political Party is 'a keystone political institution in the representative regime' **Zoya Hasan**

The Political Parties are the two way communication that binds 50 million to the 630 which in common exercise omnipotent power **Finer**

A Political party is 'an association organized in support of some principles and policies which by constitution means endeavour to make the determinant of government **R.M. Maclver**

The origins of Political parties can be traced back to the democratic revolution of the late 18th and early 19th centuries. Political parties are biased as they are committed to one ideology and oppose the ideologies and programs of their rivals. Their membership and programme reflect fundamental social divisions like class, religion, region and nationality.

Classification of Political Parties:-

Depending upon the number of political parties functioning in a country, political parties are divided into three types; One Party System, Two Party System and Multiparty System.

a. **One Party System:** It is that type of party system in which there is only one single party in the country and there is no other party in its opposition. There may be ban on other parties due to ideological differences as seen in communist countries or the ruler of the country is opposite to any political party as seen in Germany during time of Hitler and in Italy during times of Mussolini. In this system all other political parties are abolished in these countries. There is no difference between party and government. In contemporary times, people get a choice to choose their representative but from a single party. This system of choosing representative from a single party is famous in communist countries. Following are some of the merits of one party system.

i. It provides a stable government.
ii. It saves the expenditure from royal treasury.
iii. It is suitable for a small country.
iv. It provides better security and has less crime.
v. Italy and Germany used this party system to develop.
vi. It is suitable for corrupt and uncivilized citizens.
vii. It is better for integrity and national security of a nation.
viii. It saves time and development projects are not delayed due to absence of opposition and protest.
ix. It makes national progressive within short period of time.
x. It provides a centralised administration.

a. **Bi-Party System:** This party system is also known by the name of two party systems. In this system the sharing of power is effected only by two major parties. This system of political parties provides a choice for the voters to vote according to their choice of forming government. This system is seen in democratic countries such as America, Britain, Belgium and Ireland etc. In this system there is complete freedom for the formation of a third political party. The countries having bi-party system does not give much importance to party system and treat it as an instrument for winning elections. The formation of opposition party in the parliament is an important element which checks the functioning of government. Following are the some of the merits of two party system..

   i. It provides choice for the voters to elect.
   ii. It provides stable government.
   iii. It saves times and money.
   iv. It also provides opposition.
   v. It is followed by developed and civilized countries.
   vi. It provides rotation of government.
   vii. Every party has its ideology.
   viii. It possesses election manifesto to impress the Voters.
   ix. Discussion in parliament takes place in this system due to strong opposition.
   x. It Provides freedom to voters.

c. **Multi- Party System:** It is that system of political party in which sharing of political power for the formation of government is effected by more than two parties. This party system is more democratic as compared to two party systems. This system provides less stable government as compared to two party systems. The voters get more and more choices of voting for their government. Coalition government is also an important feature of multi party system. Due to coalition government fails many times. This party system is followed in third World democracies including India, Pakistan, Bangladesh, and Sri Lanka and also developed western countries such as France and Italy. India has over 40 political parties big or small represented in Lok Sabha over last 10 years. Following are some of the merits of multi-party system;

i. It is more democratic as compared to one or bi-party system.
ii. It provides opportunities to new parties and new candidates to come in power.
iii. It leads to coalition politics.
iv. It provides a boost to regional parties.
v. It is suitable for large countries.
vi. Every ideology gets an opportunity to glow.
vii. It gives unlimited choice to voters to vote.
viii. Every political party tries to give its best for coming to power.
ix. It offers decentralization of power.

<u>Features of Authoritative and Democratic Regime</u>

Political regime: The term regime stands for specifically institutional arrangement, how relationships are arranged, patterned and organized in a given society. The term "Political regime" denotes the particular political institutional arrangements. How political relationships are structured, and organised in a given society. A political regime embodies the set of rules, processes, and understanding that formulate the relationship between governs and the governed. In every political regime there are a variety of political institutions i.e. the legislature, the political parties and the bureaucracy that performed the allocated tasks and roles in governance.

Political regimes in modern time can be classified as democratic regime, traditional regime and authoritarian regime.Mostly political regimes are of three types i.e. Democratic regime, Traditional Regime and Authoritarian Regime.

Authoritarian Regime: The word "Authoritarian" is derived from word authority. It is a system of governance in which the ruler derives his authority from some cause. Authoritarianism can be a result of formation of a national state. In some time, especially when some state is weak or insecure, the ruler of the day show a tendency to get authoritarian of cause in the name of acquiring strength to deal with the external forces and provide security to the nation. Hitler was one of such examples.

Authoritarianism can be result of a particular political culture of the country. It may be result of fast economic modernisation taking place in the state. In the process of modernisation, the traditional patterns of the economic and social life get disturbed and the aspiration and demands of the people are highlighted resulting in authoritarian regime.

Types of authoritarian regime: On an average about half of the political regimes in the world are based on authoritarianism. They can be classified as Tyrannies regimes, Dynastic regimes, Military Regimes and Single Party regimes. These are explained below.

a. **Tyrannies:** In these political regimes, political power is acquired and welded by a tyrant in a personal and absolute manner. The instrument of coercion is carefully developed through police and army to maintain peace and order and revolution. Through usual services such as public health, transportation, law and order etc. Are delivered in such regime e.g. Somoza in Nicaragua, Batista in Cuba, Bokassa in Central Africa etc.

b. **Dynastic Regime:** In this type of regime political power is not acquired on the bases of force, it is held by king family. In dynastic regime the power of the king tempered by immemorial customs, conviction, understanding and religious standards. The wealth of the nation is the whim of the king there is lack of political participation of the citizen. Only an elite class which too, the kith and kin of king participate in political affair. Some of these dynastic regimes are changing into constitutional regime such as in Nepal and Morocco.

c. **Military Regime:** Military government is one of the most important contemporary regimes particularly in the third world countries. In order to maintain law and order in a state, there is need of police and army. If of army works under the democratic rules it is known a democratic regime. Some time the army reveals over the elected regime as a result of constitutional failure. This is known as military regime. The military regime of 1991 in Pakistan under General Parveez Mushraf is a good example of it. '

d. **Single Party Authoritarian Regime:** In such regime the single party is the only on the organisation the regime establishes are alliance in order to maintain its rule and gains sports. Single parties are just support agencies to the government. They provide only limited channels of popular participation. Such regimes have failed to institutionalise themselves in contrast to single parties in totalitarian regime. Single party authoritarian regimes whether military or civil exist in Syria, Iraq, Tunisia and Egypt etc.

Features of Authoritative Regime:

a. State is regarded as end and individual as means.
b. It is opposite to the democratic regime.
c. People have no role in decision making process.
d. Ideology of the ruler is the ideology of state.
e. The basis of authority is force.
f. Ruler controls total life of individuals.
g. It has no faith in international rules and regulations.
h. There is no independence of Judiciary.
a. Legislative, executive and Judiciary functions in a single person or a body of person.
j. There is centralization of power.
k. There is no opposition.
ax. There is no protest of development projects.
all. It is good for becoming a nuclear power state.
n. Its failure can lead to democratic regime.
o. It saves election expenditure.

Democratic Regimes: A democratic society is assumed to be free. Its citizens are free to elect the government for a fixed time.

The entire democratic regimes have a constitution, short or detailed or written or convention based. The citizens were also responsible and the government is also accountable for the citizen by means of periodical elections and question answer in house. Some democratic countries even provide referendum, plebiscite etc. to provide more power to their citizens.

The constitution clearly mentioned the specific roles and power which are assigned to the three organs of the government i.e. Legislative, executive and judiciary. Some constitution makes a mentioned of political party, army and other bodies such as in communist countries.

The nature of executive in a democratic regime can be either in a presidential type such as in the USA or a parliamentary type such as in India or it may be a combination of these two such as in France. In parliamentary form of democratic regime, legislative enjoys supreme power to makes laws, make appointments, control financial and dismissal of head of government i.e. PM and his ministers. In parliamentary type of regime the cabinet is headed by PM and commands supreme political power.

In Presidential type of democracy, the President is head of the state as well as government. There is separation of power between President and the parliament. There is a system of check and balance. This system is present in USA.

In the mixture of Presidential and parliamentary form of the President holds the executive power, he is the head of the state and in the same time he is also the head of his cabinet. This system is known as same Presidential and semi parliamentary regime. This system of political regime is represented in France.

Participation and timely elections are the two basic element of democratic regime. In this system there is participation of all the citizens in the election. This participation decides the formation of government by the power of their vote. So in democracy the citizens are held with the power of judgment by means of elections.

Features of Democratic Regime:

a. The citizens enjoy the universal adult Franchise.
b. The ruler holds the power for a fixed period.
c. Citizens enjoy various rights.
d. It involves functional specialization.
e. Legislative, executive and Judiciary functions within the limits set by constitution or law.
f. Government is accountable to the public.
g. Currently it is the best practicable system of governance.
h. Political parties are important organ of Democratic Regime.
a. It provides higher degree of Administrative efficiency.
j. Every government tries its best so that it can again come in power.

Keys to Remember

i. Functional representation was advocated by G D H Cole
v. Single Transferable vote system was advocated by Carl Andrae
v. Instructed representation was advocated by Montesquieu
v. In Australia, Belgium etc. there is compulsory voting.
v. J S Mill supported open ballot voting.
v. Bentham supported secret voting system.
v. Inside the Indian parliament there is open ballot voting.
v. Second ballot system is used in France.
v. Limited Votes plan is used for election to lower houses in Italy and Japan.
v. Conservative theory of representation was advocated by Edmund Burk and James Madison.
v. Liberal theory of Representation was advocated by John Locke and Thomson Jefferson.
v. Radical theory of representation was advocated by J. J. Rousseau.
v. National Voters day is celebrated on 25 January.
v. National Constitution day is celebrated on 26 November.

Objective Type Questions

1. Which of the following supported open ballot voting?

a. Bentham
b. J. S. Mill
c. Karl Marx
d. Hegel

2. Which of the following supported secret ballot voting?

a. J. S. Mill
b. T. H. Green
c. Jeremy Bentham
d. H. G. Hegel

3. Which of the following supported plural voting?

a. Machiavelli
b. J. S. Mill
c. T. H. Green
d. None of the above

4. Second ballot voting is popular in which of the following countries?

a. Germany
b. USA
c. India
d. France

5. Which of the following countries has compulsory voting?

a. India
b. France
c. Belgium
d. China

6. Which of the following advocated *'Functional representation'*?

a. Bentham
b. G. D. H. Cole
c. Lucian Pye
d. None of the above

7. Which among the following gave Radical theory of representation?

a. Lucian Pye
b. J. S. Mill
c. J. J. Rousseau
d. None of the above

8. Which among the following advocated the single transferable vote system?

a. Jeremy Bentham
b. Karl Marx
c. Gramsci
d. Carl Andrae

9. Open ballot voting in India is held for

a. Voting inside Indian Parliament
b. Voting in Panchayti Raj bodies
c. Voting in Muncipal bodies
d. None of the above

10. 'National Constitution day' is celebrated on?

a. 26th August
b. 26th September
c. 26th October

d. 26th November

11. Which one of the following is celebrated as *'National voters day'*

a. 25th January
b. 26th February
c. 26th August
d. None of the above

12. Which one of the following belongs to British Labour Party?

a. Jeremy Bentham
b. James Mill
c. J. J. Rousseau
d. James Stuart Mill

13. In a democracy, each adult citizen must have

a. Must have one vote
b. Each vote must have one value
c. A and B
d. None of the above

14. In Saudi Arabia women got the right to vote?

a. 2013
b. 2014
c. 2015
d. 2016

15. Which country has never been under a military or dictatorship rule?

a. Cuba
b. Mexico

c. India
d. Nepal

16. Who was the founder of Bhujan Samaj Party?

a. Sahu Maharaj
b. Jyotiba Phule
c. B. R. Ambedkar
d. Kanshi Ram

17. Which party believes in Marxism-Leninism?

a. Communist Party of India
b. Nationalist Congress Party
c. Bhujan Samaj Party
d. Indian National Congress

18. Which of the following country has multiparty system?

a. India
b. USA
c. UK
d. China

19. Which among the following countries has two party system/

a. UK
b. China
c. India
d. Oakistan

20. Which among the following is considered as the best form of government?

a. Democracy

b.   Monarchy
c.   Dictatorship
d.   Military Rule

Answer key
1. (b) 2. (c) 3. (b) 4. (d) 5. (c) 6. (b) 7. (c) 8. (d) 9. (a) 10. (d) 11. (a)
12. (d) 13. (a) 14. (c) 15. (b) 16. (d) 17. (a) 18. (a) 19. (a) 20. (a)

CHAPTER FOUR

Emerging issues in comparative politics

Globalization: Meaning, Nature and Evolution

Globalization: It is a process by which the whole world is so connected socially and economically such that it is like a village. It can be described as the widening, deepening and spreading up of worldwide interconnectedness in all aspects of contemporary social and political life.

Definitions:

Doubling of space and time, emphasising this with instantaneous communication, knowledge and culture, which can be shared around the world simultaneously *Anthony Giddens*

Evolution of Globalization: A pattern of interconnectedness has always existed since the rise of modern state in the fifteenth century, due to war, trade etc. Internal politics has been effected by international events and developments and interdependence of state has been stressed upon. However what we are experiencing today is a qualitatively new phenomenon. Vast networks of global interaction and financial flow over which individual states have very limited control, tremendous growth in communication, emergence of international organisation, regimes, trans governmental action and global military etc.

The seeds of globalisation were sown in the early eighties itself as many concession were granted to foreign capital. Multi-national corporations (MNC) were allowed to enter in a number of crucial sectors. However the real boost to globalisation was provided by new economic policy introduced by the government through IMF and World Bank.

Globalisation is the end product of a historical process of expansion of capitalism. The first great expansion of Europe capitalism took place in 16th century but the first major expansion of world trade and investment took place in late 19th century following the industrial revolution in Europe.

The Second World War brought another great expansion of capitalism with the rise of multi-national companies which internationalised product and trade. In the economic field, the new Breton world system helped in the rise of international financial market. In political terms, decolonisation created a new world order with emergence of a number of new states.

With the fall of Berlin Wall and Collapse of USSR, capitalism has increased with its influence with this globalisation has become a reality for the people with the living in all spheres of world. With the help of internet and social media such as Face-book, Twitter, WhatsApp and YouTube etc the Wold is so much connected such that it looks like a global village. In India globalisation has stated in real sense in 1991 when Narshima Rao government applied the system of LPG i.e. Liberalisation, Privatization, Globalisation.

Feature of Globalisation: Following are the feature of globalisation.

a. **Global Connectivity:** With the help of Globalisation we are so much connected that we can learn different languages from internet, spread over culture and learn about different things.

b. **Global Moment:** It helps us in spreading freedom movement from one part of world to another. Such as political freedom movement and women empowerment moment etc.

c. **Competitive Economy:** With globalisation every economies is competing with one another so that it could survive in global world.

d. **Spread of MNC's:** With the coming of the MNC's the cost of the things has reduced which directly help the poor section of the people to improve their livelihood.

e. **Interconnected Economy:** In this globalisation world the economies of the world are inter connected, rise of fall in price of dollar, rise and fall in crude oil prices has a worldwide impact.

<u>Women's Issues: Welfare to Empowerment</u>

Women Issues: The position of women in different Societies is different, but one thing is common that in every society they are dominated by their male partners. In almost all the societies they were given very less importance. In developed countries of the west, women are in a little bit good position but they are supposed to be weak as compare to male.

During the election campaign of US President, Hillary Clinton was supposed to be weak before the Donald Trump and this was the main reason she was defeated in election of President Candidate. In ancient India, women were respected as mother, sister and daughters. They were treated as Goddess. With the passage of time and frequent invasions by invaders, they lost their respect in the society.

During the Mahabharata, *Drupadi* was divided by *Pandas* as common wife and also miss behaved by *Kauroes*. In modern India too, the condition of women is not good. The *Shah Bano* case, *Nirbhaya* rape case etc are its live examples. India is one of the top most countries having women insecurity. National commission for women in India released a data in 2015 showing that half of the rape cases in India are from the state of Utter Pradesh.

In addition to this Indian's women were not weak. India is a home of various lioness women such as late Miss Vijay Lakshmi Pandit, Late Miss Indra Gandhi, Late Mother Terisa, Late Kalpna Chawla, Mrs Sonia Gandhi, Miss Sunita William and Mrs Patiba Devi Singh Patal.

Following are the some of the women issues:

a. **Issue of Child Marriage:** Today also female are being married much before their maturity. It results in increase in the population of country and the bad condition of women in society.

b. **Issue of polygamy:** The women in India are also affected badly by the polygamy. Now a day women in Muslim as well as tribal community are facing this problem.

c. **Right to Divorce:** Govt. of India has passed *Tripple Talaq* Bill restricting more than one marriage and making diverse a tough process for Muslim communities.

d. **Issue of Dowry:** It a major cause for poverty in various states of India such as Utter Pradesh, Bihar, Gujarat and Rajasthan etc. The Govt. has failed to check this ill practice in Society.

e. **Issue of Right to Property:** In this Patriarchal Society women are denied property rights. With this they get no share in the property of her parents.

f. Continuous Rapes in India: This is a matter of shame for a country whose history clearly shows that females were worshiped in the form of Goddess. Today girls are not safe outside their homes in any corner of India. Nirbhaya rape case in Delhi and Gudia rape case of Shimla etc. are some of its live examples. The condition has become so worse that even female animals such as Bitch, Goat etc. are not safe in India.

Some of the positive steps for women empowerment are given below;

a. **Sati was abolished in 1829:** It is seen as a major development in the path of women empowerment

b. **Bharat street Maha mandal:** It is a self help group made by women. This group has played an important role in the development of women in India.

c. **Women Indian association 1917:** It is also a self help group made by women. This group has also played an important role in the development of women in India.

d. **All India women conference 1927:** It is a Non-Governmental Organization formed by Margaret Cousins at Delhi in 1927. It has worked more for education of women and children.

e. **National Commission for women 1990:** It is a statutory body of Government of India. Its main aim is to advise the government on all policy matters affecting women.

From Welfare to Empowerment: 42nd amendment in 1976 added a fundamental duty for dignity of women in art 51A. National policy for improvement of women was formed in 2001. In 16th Lok Sabha elections, 61 women were elected. The women stated their journey by demanding for their welfare but today they are struggling for empowerment.

Following are some of the points claiming for their demands of empowerment.

a. **Entry in Sabrimala Temple:** This temple is situation in Kerala. Women from the reproductive age group were not allowed to visit this temple. In 2006 six women filled a petition to lift the ban against entering of 10 – 50 years age women. In 2018 Supreme Court of India agreed on it.

b. *Mee Too* **Movement:** It is a social movement against the sexual abuse and sexual harassment where people publicize allegation of sex crime committed with them. Women mostly avoid disclosing any misbehaved incident with them to anybody due to cultural curtains particularly in India. *Mee Too* movement clearly shows the confidence of women to publicize allegation of sex crime committed with them.

c. *Tripple Talaq* **Movement:** Various women started protesting against this *Tripple Talaq* malpractice in Muslim Community. The Government was forced to take action and as a result of which Govt. of India passed *Tripple Talaq* Bill.

d. **Women in Army, Navy and Air force:** Today women are performing well in all three branches of Indian Defence forces. Women have got permanent commission even in Indian Army.

They are flying the fighter jets equally with men Pilots.

e. **Reservation for women in PRI bodies:** After the 33% reservation for women in Panchayati Raj Institutions various women are taking part in PRI politics. With this they have become more aware and empowered.

f. Women at International Level: Indian Women are shining ranging from Space to Sports. Astronuants such as Sunita William, Lt. Kalpna Chawla & Sports persons such as Shakshi Malik, Merry Com etc. are its live examples.

Climate Change: A Comparative Perspective of North and South

Climate Change: The climate of this earth is changing at a piece rate on an average prediction; there is 0.3% degree Celsius increase per decade in global temperate over the next century. The carbon dioxide in the atmosphere has risen by about 25% in the last 150 years. With this increase in temperature the glacier is melting resulting in increase in the sea level as a global problem, this need a global solution. During the phase of industrialization the developed countries developed themselves by polluting the environment as a result of which today environmental so much polluted.

The framework on which global action on climate change may tack place was defined in the United Nation frame work Convention on Climate Change (UNFCC) in 1992 and later in Tokyo Protocol. In spite of being a step in the positive directions, it has been made imperfect as some of world largest polluters have stayed out of the convention and some amount those how have joined have demanded and received changes that has weaken the protocol considerably.

Comparative Perspective of North and South: The north consists of industrialized developed and rich countries. The South consists of the developing countries. The north world just 20% of the world pollution but consumes 80% of the world energy. The South on the other hand is still struggling to provide basic needs of the food, water, shelter, clothing, basic education and health for its population. The south world is doing following things for their survival.

a. Use of forest wood for fuel.
b. Lack of agriculture by growing population.
c. Large population living in unhealthy manner.

All these factors directly or indirectly affect the ecology and environment. The southern countries are not financially strong so as to purchase clean technologies, use manufacturing technologies which adversely affect the environment.

The North countries which consume the 80% of the global energy are responsible for the problem facing the planet today. The North-South divide issue is thus a problem which requires an urgent solution. The only solution is that the north should help the south by providing eco-friendly green technology that too with free of costs so that the south could not pollute the environment and live a sustainable life. Not only government but civil societies and NGO's could play a good role in it.

Human Rights: Meaning, Significance and Trends

Human Rights: Human Rights are those conditions of life that allows us to develop and use our human qualities of intelligence and conscience and to satisfy our spiritual needs. We cannot develop our personality in their absence. They are fundamental to our nature, without them we cannot live as human beings. These are those conditions which the state should provide to every citizen in order that they may attain their best self in society.

The idea of human right is as old as state. We may find city state system in Greek, Roman Empire in Europe, Confucian system in China, Islamic political system in Muslims countries and Panchayati Raj system in India. The concept of rights in above system was not fully developed but its origin can easily be traced here. What today we have is the development of these basic concepts in full sense.

Many important revolutions and evolutions contributed to the development of humans rights. Earlier among them we have Magna

Carta of 1215, the Petition of Rights 1628 and the Bill of Rights 1689. These three documents were from the United Kingdom and can be treated as the origin of modern human rights. After this Virginia declaration of rights 1776, The American declaration of Independence 1776, French declaration of rights of men and citizens 1789 and series of amendments to the US constitution adopted in 1791 as American Bill of rights also contributed much to development of human rights.

While the British, American and French documents gradually elaborated important civil and political rights, the October revolution of soviet Russia in 1917 brought to forefront of social, economic and cultural rights. The Socialists revolution left a lasting impact on developing a new concept of human rights that recognized economic, social and cultural rights as human rights.

The impact of socialist revolution is clearly seen in the drafting of many international human right treaties under the banner of the United Nation. With the establishment of the UN in 1945 the process of evolving and 'international bill of rights' began. In 1948 it adopted the Universal Declaration of Human Rights which included both Civil, Political and Economic social rights in a single document.

Since the universal declaration is not a legal binding document, so UN adopted to new convention in 1966. These new convention are one on civil and political rights, other on economic, social and culture rights. These are legally binding on drafting states. Thus human right has been internationalised and there are available to every human being whenever he lives.

Objective Type Questions

1. Who said "Globalization has become a necessity and there is no escape from it"?

a. Brack Obama
b. Donald Trump
c. Narindera Modi

d. Bill Clinton

1. What is the full form of LPG?

a. Liberation of particular group
b. Liberalization Privatization Globalization
c. Limited Private Group
d. None of the Above.

3. India adopted the concept of LPG in which of the following year?

a. 1988
b. 1989
c. 1990
d. 1991

4. Who was the prime Minister of India during the LPG adaptation?

a. Atal Bihari Vajpai
b. Narinder Modi
c. V. P. Singh
d. Narshima Rao

5. What is the full form of IPCC?

a. Indian Panel Code Conduct
b. Intergovernmental Panel on Climate Change
c. Indian governmental panel on climate change
d. None of the above

6. National Commission for Women was established in which of the following year?

a. 1997
b. 1990
c. 1994
d. None of the above

7. Which of the following was the first president of UN General Assembly?

a. Mrs. Vijay Lakshmi Pandit
b. Mrs. Sarojni Naidu
c. Mrs. Indera Gandhi
d. None of the above

8. Which one of the following won silver medal in wrestling?

a. Depika Padukon
b. Sakshi Malik
c. Sunita William
d. None of the above

9. Self employed Women Association (SEWA) was established by which of the following?

a. Margaret Cousins
b. Sarla Devi
c. Ela Bhat
d. None of the above

10. 'Chipko Movement' is related to which of the following states/ Union Territories?

a. Utter Pradesh
b. Jammu and Kashtmir
c. Leh
d. Uttrakhand

11. Which of the following women is known for '*Chipko Movement*'?

   a. Zaya Hassan
   b. Sanya Mirza
   c. Gaura Devi
   d. None of the above

12. United Nations General Assembly adopted Universal Declaration of Human Right on?

   a. 10th December, 1948
   b. 12th December, 1948
   c. 13th December, 1948
   d. None of the above

13. '*The Rights of Man*' was written by which of the following writers?

   a. J. S. Mill
   b. Thomas Paine
   c. Jeremy Bentham
   d. None of the above

14. Which of the following king gave "*Magna Karta*" a human rights document was in 1215?

   a. Louis IV of France
   b. King John
   c. Alexander the Great
   d. None of the above

Answer key

1. (a) 2. (b) 3. (d) 4. (d) 5. (b) 6. (b) 7. (a) 8. (b) 9. (c) 10. (d) 11. (c) 12. (a) 13. (b) 14. (b)

CHAPTER FIVE

Old papers

BA IV Semester CBCS – IIIs/12

Political Science Course No.: USPSTC - 401

Time Allowed 2 12 Maximum Marks: 80

Note: The question paper consists of three sections.

Section - A

This section includes five compulsory short answer type questions. Each question in this section is of 3 marks to be answered in 70-80 words. **(5X3 = 15)**

1. Define the term of Comparative Politics?
2. Discuss the types of Political Culture?
3. Explain concept of the 'Iron Law of Oligarchy'
4. Write any three merits of the One Party System.
5. Elaborate the concept of Globalization.

Section B

This section consists of five compulsory medium answer type questions. Each question in this section is of 7 marks to be answered in 250 - 300 words. **(5X7 =35)**

1. Explain the Political Economy Approach?
2. Elaborate the meaning and types of Political Participation.
3. Discuss the merits of Bi-Party System.
4. Explain the term and features of Authoritarian Regimes.
5. Analyse the emerging trends in the field of Human Rights.

Section - C

This section consists of 4 long answer type questions. The candidates have to attempt 2 out of these 4 questions with upper limit of 500 - 600 words. Each question carries 15 marks.
(2X15 = 30)

1. Examine David Easton's contribution to the System Approach.
2. Write an essay on Political Development.
3. Make a critical analysis of the Pluralist Theory of Democracy.
4. Make a comparative analysis of North and South perspective on Climate Change.

CHAPTER SIX

Important Political Thinkers

ALEXIX DE TOCQUEVILLE: He was a French aristocrat, diplomat, political scientist, political philosopher and historian. He is best known for his works *Democracy in America* and *The Old Regime and the Revolution* (1856). In both, he analyzed the improved living standards and social conditions of individuals as well as their relationship to the market and state in Western societies. *Democracy in America* was published after Tocqueville travel in the United States and is today considered an early work of sociology and political science. From 1839 to 1851, he served as Member of the Lower house of Parliament.

DAVID EASTON: He was born in 1917 in Canada and then took American Citizenship. He was a Political Scientists. He served as professor of Political Science at Chicago University. He is well known for his *Political System Theory*. He died in 2014.

DAVID APTER: He was an American political scientist and sociologist. He was Professor of Comparative Political and Social Development and Senior Research Scientist at Yale University. He was born in 1924. He taught at Northwestern University, the University of Chicago, the University of California, and Yale University. He was elected a Fellow of the American Academy of Arts and Sciences in 1966. He was a Guggenheim Fellow, a visiting fellow at All Souls College, Oxford, a Fellow of the Institute for Advanced Study in Princeton, New Jersey, a Fellow of the Center for Advanced Study in the Behavioral Sciences in Palo Alto, California, a Fellow of the Netherlands Institute for Advanced Study, as well as a Phi Beta Kappa Lecturer. In 2006 he was the first recipient of the Foundation Mattei Dogan prize for contributions to Interdisciplinary research. He died in his home in North Haven.

EDWARD SHILS: (1910 – 1995) he was a Distinguished Service Professor in the Committee on Social Thought and in Sociology at the University of Chicago and an influential sociologist. He was known for his research on the role of intellectuals and their relations to power and public policy. His work was honored in 1983 when he was awarded the Balzan Prize. In 1979, he was selected by the National Council on the Humanities to give the Jefferson Lecture, the highest award given by the U.S. federal government for distinguished intellectual achievement in the humanities.

FRANK THAKURDAS: He was from the famous Thakurdas family of Lahore and fondly referred to as *"Uncle"* by his students and junior colleagues was one of the most admired teachers who taught **western philosophy and drama.** Associated with the **Kirori Mal College** and the Political Science department, "Uncle" was a major influence in the lives of so many. Cine star **Amitabh Bachchan**, actors, **Kulbhushan Kharbanda, T.P. Jain, V.M. Badola** and **Shyam Arora** were all his disciples.

FRIEDRICH WILHELM NIETZSCHE: Born on 15 October 1844, Nietzsche grew up in the town of Röcken (now part of Lützen), near Leipzig, in the Prussian Province of Saxony. He was named after King Friedrich Wilhelm IV of Prussia, who turned 49 on the day of Nietzsche's birth in 1869, Nietzsche received an offer to become a professor of classical philology at the University of Basel in Switzerland. He was only 24 years old and had neither completed his doctorate nor received a teaching certificate. He was awarded an honorary doctorate by Leipzig University in March 1869. ***The Gay Science, God is Dead*** and **will to power** are his best published articles.

GABRIEL ALMOND: Gabriel Almond: He was an American Political Scientist best known for his work on Comparative Politics,

Political Development and Political Culture. He was born in USA in 1911. He was an educator at Chicago University. He died in 2002 in USA. His notable work is *The Civic Culture* 1963.

GIOVANI SARTOORI: He was born in Florence in 1924 and graduated in Political and Social Sciences from the *University of Florence* in 1946. He became a lecturer in Modern Philosophy (1950–56) and in Political Science (1956–63), and subsequently professor of Sociology (1963–66) in University of Florence. He became full professor of Political Science and taught at Florence University from 1966 to 1976. He also taught at the European University Institute (1974–76) and then became professor of Political Science at *Stanford University* (1976–79). Finally, He served as Albert Schweitzer Professor in the Humanities at *Columbia University* from 1979 to 1994. His popular work is *'Parties and Party Systems: A Framework for Analysis'*.

G. BINGHAM POWELL: He was born in 1942 in USA. He is a professor of Political Science in the University of Rochester. He also served as President of American Political Science Association. He has worked with Gabriel Almond. Their famous works are Comparative Politics: A Developmental Approach and Comparative Politics Today.

HAROLD D LASSWELL: (1902 – 1978) was an American political scientist and communications theorist. He earned his bachelor's degree in philosophy and economics and was a PhD student at the *University of Chicago*. He was a professor of law at *Yale University*. He studied at the *Universities of London*. He served as president of the *American Political Science Association* (APSA), of the *American Society of International Law* and of the *World Academy of Art and Science* (WAAS). Lasswell is well known for his *model of communication*, which focuses on "*Who (says) What (to) Whom (in) What Channel (with) What Effect*". He is also known for his book on on politics, *Politics: Who Gets What, When, and How.*

JEAN BLONDEL: He was born in 1929. He is a French political scientist with specialization in comparative politics. He is currently

Emeritus Professor at the European University Institute in Florence, and visiting professor at the University of Siena. He lives in London. His work has focused recently in a comparison of different presidential systems across the globe, with a particular emphasis on Latin America, Africa and the ex-Soviet republics. It seeks to be amongst the first comprehensive studies of different presidential systems. His new book is "***Presidents and Democracy in Latin America***" edited with Manuel Alcantara and Jean-Louis Thiebault. *'An Introduction to Comparative Government'* is also one of his popular works.

JAMES SAMUEL COLEMAN: He was born in 1926 and died in 1995. He was an American sociologist, theorist, and empirical researcher, based chiefly at the University of Chicago. He was elected president of the American Sociological Association in 1991. He studied the sociology of education and public policy, and was one of the earliest users of the term social capital. His Foundations of Social Theory influenced sociological theory. His The Adolescent Society (1961) and "Coleman Report" (Equality of Educational Opportunity, 1966) were two of the most cited books in educational sociology.

JAMES BRYCE: He was born in 1838 and died in 1922. He was a British academic, jurist, historian, and Liberal politician. He was having his specialization in law, government, and history. This expertise led him to high political offices culminating with his successful role as ambassador to the United States, from 1907 to 1913. His intellectual influence was greatest in *The American Commonwealth* (1888), an in-depth study of American politics that shaped the understanding of America in Britain and in the United States as well. In 1880 Bryce, an ardent Liberal in politics was elected to the House of Commons as member for the constituency of Tower Hamlets in London. In 1885 he was returned for South Aberdeen and he was re-elected there on succeeding occasions. He remained a Member of Parliament until 1907. He also wrote *Modern Democracies* in 1922.

JAMES WILFORD GARNER: He was born in 1871 in USA and died in 1938. He was alumni of *Chicago University* and *Colombia University*. He was professor of political science at the *University of Pennsylvania* in 1902–1903 and professor of political science at the *University of Illinois*, and he was editor in chief of the *American Journal of Criminal Law and Criminology* (1910–1911). He edited Essays on *Southern History and Politics* (1914). He was *Hyde lecturer* in the French universities (1921) and *Tagore lecturer* in the *University of Calcutta* (1922). His important works are *Introduction to Political Science* (1910), *Government in the United States, National, State, and Local* (1911) and *Civil Government for Indian Students* (1920).

KARL WOLFGANG DEUTSCH: He was born in 1912 and died in 1992. He was a social and political scientist from Prague. He was a professor at MIT, Yale University and Harvard University An influential 20th century social scientist, Deutsch studied war and peace, nationalism, co-operation, and communication, as well as pioneered quantitative methods and formal system analysis and model-thinking into the field of political and social sciences. '*The Nerves of Government: Models of Political Communication and Control*' is his famous work.

LUCIAN PYE: He was born in China in 1921. He took American Citizenship. He was a well known Political Scientist well known for his work in *Sociology & Comparative Politics*. He was a faculty at *Wale University*.

MYRON WEINER: He was born in 1931 in America. He was an American Political Scientist & renowned Scholar of India, South Asia, Ethnic Movement & Child Labour etc. He was a student of Massachusetts Institute of Technology (MIT) USA. His publication '*The Child and the State in India: Child Labour and Education Policy in Comparative Politics*' is very popular. He has worked on state politics in India particularly party system and ethnic conflict.

Michael Joseph Oakeshott: He was born in 1901 and died in 1990. He was an English philosopher and political theorist who wrote about philosophy of history, philosophy of religion, aesthetics, philosophy of education, and philosophy of law. He published his first book in 1933, Experience and its Modes, when he was thirty-one. He acknowledged the influence of Georg Wilhelm Friedrich Hegel and F. H. Bradley. Commentators also noticed resemblances between this work and the ideas of thinkers such as R. G. Collingwood and Georg Simmel. Rationalism in Politics and Other Essays (1962), On Human Conduct and On Being Conservative (1956) are his important works.

ROBERT DAHL: Robert Alan Dahl was born in 1915 in USA and died in 2014. He was an American political theorist and Sterling Professor of Political Science at Yale University. He established the pluralist theory of democracy—in which political outcomes are enacted through competitive, if unequal, interest groups—and introduced "*Polyarchy*" as a descriptor of actual democratic governance. An originator of "empirical theory" and known for advancing behavioralist characterizations of political power, Dahl's research focused on the nature of decision making in actual institutions, such as American cities. He is the most important scholar associated with the pluralist approach to describing and understanding both city and national power structures. During World War II, Dahl enlisted in the army infantry and led a platoon that took part in a major offensive in November 1944. He was elected president of the American Political Science Association in 1966. Dahl was married to Mary Bartlett until her passing and then to Anne Sale, a Presbyterian. In his later writing, Dahl examined democracy, in particular in the United States, with a critical view. In How Democratic Is the American Constitution? (2001), Dahl argued that the US Constitution is much less democratic than it ought to be, given that its authors were operating from a position of "profound ignorance" about the future. However, he adds that there is little or nothing that can be done about this "short of some constitutional breakdown, which I neither foresee nor, certainly, wish for". In On Political Equality (2006), Dahl addresses the issue of equality and discusses how and why governments have fallen short of their democratic ideals. He assesses the contemporary political landscape in the United States.

ROY C MACRIDIS: Prof. Roy C. Macridis was a retired political scientist at Brandeis University, died on Dec. 20 at New England Deaconess Hospital in Boston. He was 72 years old and lived in Belmont, Mass. He died of cancer, an announcement from Brandeis said. A former head of the politics department, the Social Science Council and the Faculty Senate, he retired two years ago as Lawrence Wien Professor of International Cooperation. He joined the Brandeis faculty in 1965 after teaching government and political science courses at other universities, including Harvard and Columbia, starting in the late 1940's. Professor Macridis was a native of Istanbul, Turkey, and a graduate of Athens College in Greece and the University of Paris Law School, with a Ph.D. from Harvard. He worked for the Office of Strategic Services in World War II and came to this country in 1944. He wrote nine books and numerous articles on French politics, comparative politics and public policy. His "Contemporary Political Ideologies" (Little, Brown, 1983) will go to its fifth edition next year.

R H TAWNEY: He was born in 1880 in Calcutta India and died in 1962. He was an English economic historian, social critic, ethical socialist, Christian socialist and important proponent of adult education. He was the son of the Sanskrit scholar Charles Henry Tawney. During the First World War, he served as a Sergeant in the 22nd Manchester Regiment. From 1917 to 1931, he was a lecturer at the London School of Economics. His important work is The Acquisitive Society.

SAMUEL E FINER: Professor Samuel Edward Finer was born in 1915 in UK and died in 1993. He was a political scientist and historian specializing in comparative politics, who was instrumental in advancing political studies as an academic subject in the United Kingdom, pioneering the study of UK political institutions. His most notable work is The History of Government from the Earliest Times – a three-volume comparative analysis of all significant government systems. He was also a major contributor to the study of civil–military relations with the publication of his book, The Man on Horseback. His popular work The History of Government from the Earliest Times, is a comparative analysis of government systems, past and present.

SAMUEL H BEER: Samuel Hutchison Beer was born in 1911 and died in 2009. He was an American political scientist who specialized in the government and politics of the United Kingdom. He was a longtime professor at Harvard University and served as president of the Americans for Democratic Action in the early 1960s. He wrote speeches for President Franklin D. Roosevelt. He also was a reporter for The New York Post and Fortune. During World War II, Beer served in the United States Army artillery and was awarded a Bronze Star for his heroism during the D-Day Normandy landings. After the war, he was part of the Allied Military Government in Germany and eventually left the Army with the rank of captain.

SIDNEY VERBA: Sidney Verba was born in 1932 and died in 2019. He was an American political scientist, librarian and library administrator. His academic interests were mainly American and comparative politics. He was the Professor at Harvard University and also served Harvard as the director of the Harvard University Library from 1984 to 2007. Verba was educated at Harvard College and Princeton University, and served on the faculty of Princeton, Stanford University, and the University of Chicago and finally joined Harvard, where he would spend the rest of his career. The Civic Culture: Political Attitudes and Democracy in Five Nations, Equality in America: A View from the Top Cambridge and Participation in America: Political Democracy and Social Equality are his important works.

TALCOTT PERSON: He was born in America in 1902. He was an American Sociologist of the classical tradition, best known for his social action theory and Structural Functionalism. Pearson is considered as one of the most influential figure in sociology in 20th Century. He died in 1979 in Germany.

VERNON VAN DYKE: He was born in 1912 and died May 26, 1998. He graduated from Manchester College in Indiana in 1933, and he received his Ph.D. in 1937 from the University of Chicago. He served in the United States Navy during World War II. Before and after the war, he taught variously at Manchester, DePauw, Yale, and Reed College, and in summer terms at Berkeley, Columbia, and Wisconsin. He especially distinguished the faculty of the department of political science at the University of Iowa, which he joined in 1949 and from which he retired in 1983. He served as director of American Journal of Political Science. Political Science: A Philosophical Analysis.

MAX WEBER: Maximilian Karl Emil Weber was born in 1864 and died in 1920. He was a German sociologist, historian, jurist, and political economist regarded as among the most important theorists of the development of modern Western society. His ideas profoundly influence social theory and research. While Weber did not see himself as a sociologist, he is recognized as one of the fathers of sociology along with Auguste Comte, Karl Marx, and Émile Durkheim. Weber is also known for his thesis combining economic sociology and the sociology of religion, emphasizing the importance of cultural influences embedded in religion as driving factors of capitalism. This is in contrast to Marx's historical materialism, which considers religion as derivative of capitalism. After the First World War, Weber was among the founders of the liberal German Democratic Party. He also ran unsuccessfully for a seat in parliament and served as advisor to the committee that drafted the ill-fated democratic Weimar Constitution of 1919. After contracting Spanish flu, he died of pneumonia in 1920. He served as professor in Wilhelm University. He is famous for his works on bureaucracy. Legal-Rational Model of Bureaucracy was also given by him.

P M HASS: Peter M. Haas was born in 1955. He was a professor of Political Science at the University of Massachusetts Amherst and the Karl Deutsch Visiting Professor in Berlin. His research concerns epistemic communities, global environmental politics, multilevel governance, and the role of science in global politics. Haas received his undergraduate education from the University of Michigan and his Ph.D. in 1986 from the Massachusetts Institute of Technology. He has been at Amherst since 1987, and has held visiting positions at Yale University, Brown University, and Oxford University. His father, Ernst B. Haas, was also a notable political scientist

LEO STRAUSS: Leo Strauss was born in 1899 and died in 1973. He was a German-American political philosopher who specialized in classical political philosophy. Born in Germany to Jewish parents, Strauss later emigrated from Germany to the United States. He spent much of his career as a professor of political science at the University of Chicago, where he taught several generations of students and published fifteen books. Trained in the neo-Kantian tradition with Ernst Cassirer and immersed in the work of the phenomenologist Edmund Husserl and Martin Heidegger, Strauss established his fame with path-breaking books on Spinoza and Hobbes, then with articles on Maimonides and Farabi. In the late 1930s his research focused on the rediscovery of esoteric writing, thereby a new illumination of Plato and Aristotle, retracing their interpretation through medieval Islamic and Jewish philosophy, and encouraging the application of those ideas to contemporary political theory.

S M LIPSET: Seymour Martin Lipset was born in 1922 and died in 2006. He was an American sociologist and political scientist and also served as President of the American Political Science Association. His major work was in the fields of political sociology, trade union organization, social stratification, public opinion, and the sociology of intellectual life. He also wrote extensively about the conditions for democracy in comparative perspective. A socialist in his early life, Lipset later moved to the right, and was often considered a neoconservative. Political Man: The Social Bases of Politics is one of famous work of Lipset.

SAMUEL PHILLIPS HUNTINGTON: He was born in 1927 and died in 2008. He was an American political scientist, adviser, and academic. He spent more than half a century at *Harvard University*, where he was *director of Harvard's Center for International Affairs*. During the presidency of *Jimmy Carter*, Huntington was the *White House Coordinator* of Security Planning for the *National Security Council*. During the 1980s Apartheid era in South Africa, he served as an adviser to P. W. Botha's Security Services. He is best known for his 1993 theory, the "*Clash of Civilizations*", of a post-Cold War new world order. He argued that *future wars would be fought not between countries, but between cultures, and that Islamic extremism would become the biggest threat to Western domination of the world*. Huntington is credited with helping to shape American views on civilian-military relations, political development, and comparative government.

G Sartori: He was an *Italian political scientist*. He was born in 1924 and died in 2017. He was famous for his work democracy, political parties and comparative politics. He was graduated in Political and Social Sciences at the *University of Florence in 1946*. He stayed on at the University of Florence, teaching History of Modern Philosophy and Doctrine of the State starting in 1946. He became a lecturer in Modern Philosophy in 1950 and of Political Science in 1956. He also became professor of Sociology in 1963. He became full professor of Political Science and taught at Florence University from 1966 to 1976. He also taught at the European University Institute (1974–76) and then became professor of Political Science at *Stanford University* (1976–79). Finally, He served as Albert Schweitzer Professor in the Humanities at *Columbia University* from 1979 to 1994 and was appointed Professor Emeritus. He was President of the Committee for Conceptual and Terminological Analysis (COCTA) of *International Political Science Association* (IPSA), the *International Sociological Association* (ISA), and the *International Social Science Council* (ISSC) from 1970 to 1979.

Nobert Weiner: He was born in USA in 1894 and died in 1964. He was an American mathematician and philosopher. He did his MA from *Carnell University* in 1911 and Ph.D. from the *Harvard University* in 1913 and he was only *19 years* at the time of his Ph.D. He was also *rejected for a position at the University of Melbourn*. He then became a professor of mathematics at the *Massachusetts*

Institute of Technology (MIT). He became an early researcher in stochastic and mathematical noise processes, contributing work relevant to electronic engineering, electronic communication, and control systems. He is considered the originator of *cybernetics*, the science of communication as it relates to living things and machines with implications for engineering, systems control, computer science, biology, neuroscience, philosophy, and the organization of society. He is credited as being one of the first to theorize that all intelligent behavior was the result of feedback mechanisms that could possibly be simulated by machines and was an important early step towards the development of modern artificial intelligence.

Michael Curtis: He is professor emeritus of political science at Rutgers University and has taught at several other institutions, including Yale University and Cornell University. He has written and edited more than fifteen books in the fields of comparative politics, political theory, and Middle East affairs.

Polybius: Polybius was born in 200 BC and died in 118 BC. He was a Greek historian of the Hellenistic period. He is noted for his work *The Histories*, which covered the period of 264–146 BC and the Punic Wars in detail. Polybius is important for his analysis of the *mixed constitution* or the *separation of powers in government*, his in-depth discussion of *checks and balances to limit power*, and his introduction of "*the people*", which influenced *Montesquieu's The Spirit of the Laws, John Locke's Two Treatises of Government*, and the *framers of the United States Constitution*.

Montesquiue: He was a French judge, historian and political philosopher. He was born in 1689 and died in 1755. He is the principal source of the *theory of separation of powers*, which is implemented in many constitutions throughout the world. He is also known for doing more than any other author to secure the place of the word despotism in the political lexicon. His anonymously published *The Spirit of Law* (1748), which was received well in both Great *Britain* and the *American colonies*, influenced the Founding *Fathers of the United States* in drafting the

U.S. Constitution.

References

1. Almond, G. A. *The Civic Culture: Political Attitudes and Democracy in Five Nations.* Princeton University Press, USA, 1963

2. Biswal, T. *Comparative Politics: Institutions and Process.* TRINTY Publication, New Delhi.

3. Gauba, O. P. *Western Political Thought.* Mayur Paperback New Delhi, 2017

4. Johari, J. C. *Comparative Politics.* Sterling Publication PVT. LTD. New Delhi, 2020.

5. Mukherjee, S. & Ramaswami, S. *A History of Political Thought.* Prentice Hall India Learning Private Limited, 2011

6. Mukhopadhyay, A. K. *Western Political Thought.* SAGE Publications, New Delhi 2020.

7. Mukherjee, S & Ramaswami, S. *Theoretical Foundation of Comparative Politics.*

8. Sharma, S. K. & Sharma, U. *Western Political Thought.* Atlantic Publication, New Delhi, 2020.

9. Sabine, G. W. *A History of Political Theory.* Oxford and IBH Publication Publication, New Delhi 2019.

10. Singh, P. & Sharma, C. *Comparative Government and Politics.* SAGE Publication, New Delhi, 2019.

11. *Western Political Thought,* IGNOU